The Woodstock Guru: Swami Satchidananda

The untold story, the inspiration, and
the legacy of the Woodstock Music Festival

Featuring the artwork of Peter Max

Integral Yoga® Publications
108 Yogaville Way
Virginia 23921 USA

Printed in the United States of America

ISBN 978-0-932040-03-9

Integral Yoga® Publications

Buckingham, Virginia, USA
integralyoga.org

Books by Sri Swami Satchidananda:

Beyond Words
The Golden Present
Heaven on Earth
Kailash Journal
To Know Your Self
Yoga Sutras of Patanjali
Enlightening Tales
Bound To Be Free
Integral Yoga Hatha
The Living Gita
Yoga Affirmations Coloring Book
The Yoga Way

Peter Max Special Cover Art Series:

Adversity and Awakening
Free Yourself
Gems of Wisdom
How to Find Happiness
Meditation
Pathways to Peace
Thou Art That
The Be-Attitudes
Everything Will Come to You
The Guru Within
The Key to Peace
Overcoming Obstacles
Satchidananda Sutras

Books about Sri Swami Satchidananda

Boundless Giving: The Life and Service of Sri Swami Satchidananda
The Master's Touch
Sri Swami Satchidananda: Apostle of Peace

Biographical DVDs

Living Yoga: The Life and Teachings of Swami Satchidananda
Many Paths, One Truth: The Interfaith Message of Swami Satchidananda

For complete listing of books, CDs and DVDs: shakticom.org

Contents

Acknowledgments

To Sri Swami Satchidananda we offer a deep bow for the gift of his example and teachings.

Our gratitude to Conrad Rooks for recognizing a true Yoga master when he saw him and then arranging for Swami Satchidananda to come to the West in 1966.

Special thanks to Peter Max, who made it possible for Swami Satchidananda to come to America in 1966, helped establish the Integral Yoga Institute, and enabled us to utilize his brilliant artworks. Deepest thanks to Victor Arjuna Zurbel, a close friend and collaborator of Peter Max, who has dedicated his design talents to this and so many other Integral Yoga projects over many decades. Thank you to Adam Max, Libra Max, and Ann Taylor (Peter Max Studio) for their assistance and support of this and many other projects.

Our thanks to Elliott Landy for use of the color Woodstock photo of Swami Satchidananda. We appreciate Alex Figueroa and Chandra/Jo Sgammato for their editorial work on this book. Our thanks to Shiva Hervé for design/layout, Swami Hamsananda for copyediting, and Rev. Prem Anjali for project management.

Without the generosity of the Harry Wadhwani family and Rev. Sivani Alderman, this and so many other projects would not be possible. We are so grateful.

Dedication

Over the years, there have been spiritual giants who've walked this earth with heartfelt humility, spoken and acted with sensitivity and concern for all beings, without bias. Sri Swami Satchidananda was one such spiritual giant. When Swami Satchidananda first arrived in the West in 1966 and opened the Woodstock Festival in 1969, the youth of America was in need and he gave us direction, a sense of hope, and the spirit of aspiration.

To be in his loving presence felt like being in the radiant sun enveloped by a universal embrace. He was the embodiment of servicefulness and self-sacrifice. He always reminded us who we really were. He made us larger. He made us care about something greater than ourselves. By his teachings we knew that all good things were attainable. We knew that the darkness of the moment was not permanent. He showed us how our greatest challenges only helped to draw out our inner capabilities.

This book is dedicated to Swami Satchidananda and to the spirit of Woodstock, which we hope will continue to inspire generations to come.

"Let all our actions and
all our arts express Yoga.

Through that sacred art of music, let us
find peace that will pervade all over the globe.

Let us not fight for peace, but let us
find peace within ourselves first . . .

The future of the whole world is in your hands."

—Swami Satchidananda
1969 Woodstock Music Festival

The Untold Story: Being Called to Woodstock

About 100 miles north of Manhattan's Greenwich Village, steady rainfall had given rise to muddy country roads and farmland fields in the area in which the Woodstock Music and Arts Festival was to take place. A massive traffic jam was forming as more and more cars tried to approach the festival. After abandoning their vehicles, the crowds of restless youth poured onto the rented farmland; many breaking through the fencing and ignoring any attempted order. The chaos had the state police alarmed and the fate of the festival was uncertain. Michael Lang, the main festival organizer, was terrified and had to act fast. He began looking for someone to set a peaceful tone to what was quickly becoming a frightening ordeal. Lang called his friend, Peter Max and asked who he thought should open the Festival "I answered without hesitation, 'My Swami, Swami Satchidananda,'" Max recalls.

Inside his Yoga center on the West side of Manhattan , the tall, gentle Guru from India was at peace. It is mind-boggling now to think about what was about to happen—that he was about to be picked up and helicoptered into the middle of a brewing crisis. Swami Satchidananda had just finished the instruction of a Hatha Yoga class for 35 young adults, when his assistant quietly interrupted to give him the unexpected news. "Swamiji, it's Peter Max. Something about hundreds of thousands of young people at that music festival in Woodstock." (*photo: Max with his Guru.*)

Three years earlier, Max, an artist whose uniquely colorful and psychedelic paintings captured the heart of the 1960s generation, had convinced the Swami to bring his holistic form of Yoga from India to America. The Guru rested the phone against his ear and listened with his trademark meditative focus. He shook his head in agreement and replied, "Okay, Atman" (Max's Yoga name), when Max said he'd send a driver to transport the Swami to Bethel, New York.

Victor Arjuna Zurbel—a close friend of Peter Max who had helped host the Swami when he first arrived in New York—described the scene as the limo approached the festival area, "I was sitting in the center front seat. On my right, riding shotgun, was the Swami. Sitting in the back, was folk singer Tim Harden ("If I Were a Carpenter"), and two of his musicians. Despite our VIP status, we were stuck

hardly moving in the traffic caused by the festival. Eventually the traffic would be backed up for twenty miles. The driver, who was on a walkie-talkie said, 'Get ready, they're sending in a helicopter.' Sure enough, a few minutes later, a helicopter landed in the pasture, and Swamiji and I, along with Tim his bandmates, were ushered aboard."

"I truly believe that the Swami's words set the tone for that generational event when he said, 'Through the music, we can work wonders... The entire world is going to watch this. The entire world is going to know what the American youth can do to humanity.'"

—Peter Max

"On arrival, we were greeted by Lang (*below, left*) and joined the backstage group, which consisted of Richie Havens, Ravi Shankar, Melanie, Joan Baez, Arlo Guthrie, Sweetwater and The Incredible String Band. Richie Havens went on first to get everyone into the music groove before Swamiji gave his opening address. But when he did, it set the mood for a historic three days of peace and music."

My Vision: A Prequel to Woodstock

By Peter Max

It was 1966—a time of psychedelic experimentation among the youth and Yoga was virtually unknown in America. As an artist, I was on a creative retreat, experimenting with new modes of expression through the medium of collage. Before I became an artist, I had almost chosen a career as an astronomer, having had a strong fascination about the universe—planets, stars, galaxies, novas, nebulas, and the vast distances in space.

One day I decided I was going to try and find out what the universe and life were all about through my art and decided to create a large collage of the universe in my studio in New York's Upper West Side. I worked on a large table that was about five feet square and began assembling photographs. I worked on the collage for almost 16 hours a day for three days.

When it was complete, I wanted to be able to see the whole image, hoping it would give me a perspective on the universe and what life was all about. But it was so big that in order to see it, I had to climb up a ten-foot ladder and look down at it. There I was, at 2:00 a.m. in the morning, climbing a ladder up to the ceiling. When I looked down at my collage, however, I didn't really see anything that was a cosmic revelation; I was hoping to see something that was beyond belief. I was very frustrated and disappointed, especially since I had worked very hard on it.

I reached my arms up to God and wanted to scream, but suddenly realized that my wife Liz and our baby son, Adam, were asleep in the next room. So, instead, I did a kind of dry, silent scream while I closed my eyes and wished for an answer to my quest. Suddenly, with my eyes closed, I envisioned a cloud that opened up and a man with a white beard appeared through it and said, "Relax, everything is okay."

I felt a new sense of peace and began to relax as I descended the ladder. It was now 3:00 a.m. and as I was about to go to bed, my phone rang. Who could be calling me at that hour? I picked up the phone and a man said, "I'm so sorry. I'm calling from Paris and forgot the time difference. My name is Conrad Rooks." He told me that he was making a film in Paris and somebody had shown him a brochure of my collages. He loved them and asked if I could come to Paris and give him some ideas for visuals and color treatments for his film.

"When do you need me there?" I asked. He said, "I'd like you to come tomorrow." I said, "I'm sorry, I really can't. My wife just had a baby." So I said good night and went to bed. As I drifted off to sleep, all I could think about was the vision I had on the ladder of the man in the white beard.

The next afternoon, someone knocked on my door. I opened it and a man who was wearing a Zorro-style hat and a black coat that hung down to his ankles was standing there. "Hello, I'm Conrad Rooks, the man who called you last night," he said. "What are you doing here?" I exclaimed. "I thought you said you were in Paris!" "When you said you wouldn't come, I decided to get on the next plane and here I am," he declared. I invited him into the studio and when he saw my collages on the wall, he let out a loud "YAHOO," throwing his hat up to the ceiling and letting it fall to the floor.

After he looked at my art and we talked a bit, he said, "I'd like you come down and meet my friends. They're sitting on a bench across the street on Riverside Drive."

"Your friends? Who are your friends?" I asked.

"I've got Alan Ginsberg and William Burroughs waiting downstairs to tell you about my film." I couldn't believe my ears! So we went downstairs, and there sure enough was Ginsberg and Burroughs. They both told me about the extraordinary underground film that Conrad was making, *Chappaqua*. They persuaded me that the film needed my creative input and that I should go to Paris. So I decided to go.

Meeting Swami Satchidananda in Paris

When we arrived in Paris, we went to the Hotel Napoleon Bonaparte. Conrad picked up the house phone and said, "Hello, Swami? I've got the American artist with me. Can you please meet us downstairs for breakfast?" I had heard the term "Swami" before, but thought it was a man who could do special, paranormal feats and didn't know it was a monk or holy man. The elevator door opened up and a tall, dark, magnificent man walked out wearing orange clothes and a beautiful long beard. The moment I saw him, I knew that it was the man in my vision. As I shook his long, warm hand, I looked into his deep brown eyes, and was enchanted by their beauty and dynamic presence, which I realized was emanating from within. (*photo left: Chappaqua poster shoot*)

After breakfast, Conrad said, "It's time to go to see the rushes of the movie." We went to a screening room and while I watched episodes from his extraordinary film, I heard the "*OM Shanti*" chant. I had never heard any sound like that before and didn't know where it was coming from. Then the camera zoomed in on a huge banyan tree and as it panned down, I saw the Swami sitting under the

Peter Max and Conrad Rooks

tree chanting, "*Om, Shanti, Shanti, Shanti.*" I turned to look at him and he smiled back, saying, "That's me." I still had no idea what he did, but everything about him was so wonderful! The Swami left the screening a little early and I wanted to follow. I was not as interested in the film as much as I was about the Swami; I just wanted to be with him. So after the Swami left, I stayed for a few more minutes and then said to Conrad, "You know, I'm a little tired myself.

Maybe I'll go back to the hotel. By the way, what room is the Swami in?" Conrad said he was in room 776.

As soon as I entered the hotel, I went directly to the Swami's door, although I didn't want to disturb him. But as I got there, I found the door open and saw the Swami, sitting against the backboard of the bed, almost as though he was expecting me. He said, "Come, come. Come on in." I was so excited to talk with him one-on-one. I asked, "What do you do?"

"I'm a monk," he said.

"Oh, that's really nice. From India?"

"Yes, from India. But now I have an ashram in Kandy, Ceylon."

He saw that I was more than curious about the things he was telling me, so he reached up for a book on the shelf and opened it. He turned to a page that had an illustration of a person seated in lotus with a line of seven golden circles over him. He pointed to them, saying, "Those are called *chakras* and, in Yoga, we try to awaken them all. The middle one is the heart *chakra*." He continued to show me the book and I was completely fascinated. He told me about the different branches of Yoga and I asked him if he could show me a Yoga posture. He stood up straight and tall and started to demonstrate a sequence of moves. I picked up a blank envelope from the desk, and did a little drawing of each posture. I still have that envelope with the drawing.

Coming to America

We became friends and I spent the next five or six days with him. When I wasn't working with Conrad, I tried to spend every moment with the Swami to learn as much as I could from him. The last day I was in Paris, I said to him, "Swami, America needs you very, very much. It would be really nice if you could come to America." "America needs me?" he asked. "Why?" I told him that the youth were experimenting with drugs to expand their consciousness and the whole country was undergoing great change. His teachings of Yoga were what we needed. I also spoke to Conrad about bringing the Swami to America. Then the Swami told me, "Okay, if there's a need, I'll come."

I flew back to New York and when I got home, my friends all asked me to tell them about Paris and the film, but all I could talk about was the Swami. He was going to arrive three days later and I was very excited. I went to JFK airport to pick him up but missed his arriving flight and couldn't find him at the airport, so I turned around and quickly went home. When I returned to my apartment, he was already there, chatting with my wife, Liz.

She told me that when he arrived and she saw his strange clothing and unusual, long beard, she was so astonished that she quickly closed the door in his face. Then she worked up the courage to re-open it and asked, "Are you the Swami?" She was embarrassed but he gave her a beautiful heartfelt smile. When Liz and I were alone in the kitchen, she asked me what we were going to do with him, and where we could put him up. I told her that we would work it out, as he was a very great Swami. But at first, she thought it was strange that I, a 26-year-old man, with a young wife and newly born son, had brought this 52-year-old man with shoulder-length hair and a long beard into our house.

The best we could offer him to sleep on that first night was a fold-up bed in the middle of the living room, which he accepted graciously. Early the next morning, at 5:00 a.m., I had to heat up a bottle for our baby and tiptoed through the living room to get to the kitchen. As I peeked over to see if he was sleeping, I noticed that the bed was made and he was sitting in the corner in lotus pose, meditating. I was so inspired, I just had to know what this was about and wanted to learn how to do it so much. Later that day, we walked in Central Park and talked about many things. I told him about the hippies, and the new social, political and artistic movements that were happening. When we got back to my apartment, I excitedly called all my friends and invited them to come up and meet the Swami.

At six that evening about 45 people showed up. The Swami was sitting in lotus on the couch. Some of those who came in to meet him had just smoked a joint and were a little stoned; others had a cigarette in their hand. Some sat in chairs and others laid down on the floor with their legs stretched out in front of them, their feet towards the Swami (they didn't know it was considered disrespectful in the East). As the Swami started to speak in his soft, gentle voice, the people got very calm and relaxed. Those with cigarettes began to put them out and those with their legs stretched out began to sit up straight and even crossed their legs to emulate the Swami. The whole room grew very quiet and was filled with a sense of anticipation and wonder.

After speaking for about two hours, the Swami closed his eyes and silently led us into our first Yoga meditation. Afterward, we all went into the kitchen and shared our experience and discussed what we could do to keep the Swami in New York. One of my friends said, "I know what to do." He put his hands in his pockets and dropped whatever money he had on the Formica table. Everybody followed that gesture and dropped $5 and $10 bills on the table. Between us, we gathered about $100, and that was the birth of the Integral Yoga® Institute.

"Are You Hindu?" "No, I'm an Undo"

By Victor Arjuna Zurbel

Before I met Swami Satchidananda, I thought a yogi was someone who slept on a bed of nails in a side show of a carnival or something. I had no idea what it was. And when he arrived in the United States I began to learn very quickly. It just happened so extraordinarily. He taught me a new religion and that religion was called "Undo-ism." Someone once asked: "Swamiji, are you a Hindu?" And he replied, No, I'm an Un-do."

It was one wonderful lesson after another taught in a very, very special way—like my first meal with Swamiji. We went to a restaurant and I ordered a bacon, lettuce and tomato sandwich and I said, "Would you like one?" And he said, "Yes, that would be quite wonderful; just tell them to hold the bacon."

In 1966, I invited him to move into my apartment. I lived off Central Park and the Museum of Natural History was a block away; the American Historical Society was downstairs. I told him, "Swamiji, the museum is right downstairs, the park is right across the street."

He said, "That's quite alright, I'll be very happy to stay inside."

And I thought maybe he didn't want to go out.

But then, he added, "I'll be very happy to stay inside, I've been traveling around, and I have all the beautiful parks and museums within me."

At that point, I just stood there and tears rolled down my cheeks, and I didn't know what the word "Guru" was, but at that moment I knew I had a Guru. And then he explained to me what a Guru was. It's two Sanskrit syllables: *Gu* and *Ru*—remover of ignorance, which was undoism.

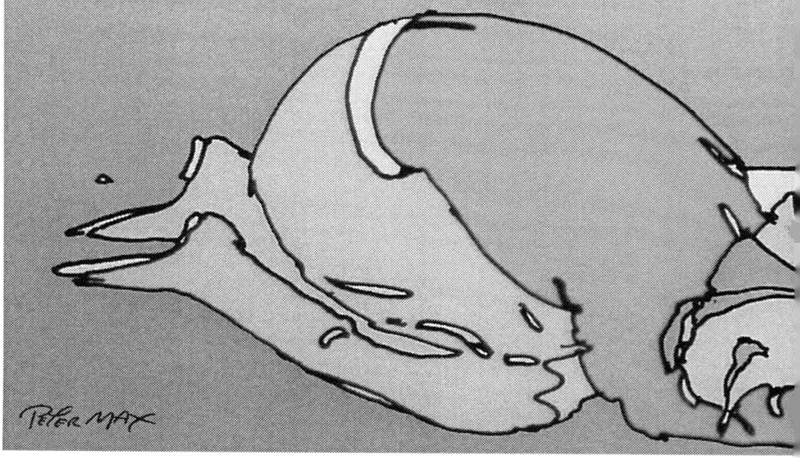

The Rest is History

In my New York City apartment those first two weeks, about 10 to 25 people would come each evening for casual lectures, and when we moved to the Oliver Cromwell Hotel only two weeks later, there were 25 to 50. And that was where Swamiji started to teach Hatha Yoga. (*Zurbel with Swamiji: page 24, far left*)

He gave the classes himself and soon the proficient students began teaching. Then when it grew larger, we incorporated the Integral Yoga Institute on October 7, 1966, and moved over to 500 West End Avenue. The rest is history.

There were many opportunities in those early days to obtain notoriety on TV and in the press, but Swamiji wisely steered away, anticipating wrong exploitation.

The Integral Yoga Institute grew like a tree. Swamiji nurtured it like a gardener, checking the condition of the soil, replanting it with care every time it grew too big for the pot, snipping off the top a little so some nice branches could come out, and when the time was right, letting it take root in a beautiful building on West 13th Street in Greenwich Village.

At 500 West End Ave., the door is open
to meet Swami Satchidananda
(And when you leave, you may find
that another door is open.)
Friday, May 15, 7-9 P.M.
500 West End Ave. (W.84th St.) Apt. 5A. Admission Free.

About a decade later, Swami Satchidananda also founded Yogaville®, a spiritual and Yoga oasis with a retreat and training center for Yoga teachers and therapists. As Peter Max recently told Forbes.com, "He wasn't the first Yoga master to come to America but, with his opening words at Woodstock and the creation of the Integral Yoga organization, he helped modern Yoga take firm roots here, and introduced it to thousands, if not millions of people in the West." Author Philip Goldberg agrees, "The image of Swami Satchidananda at Woodstock will always be a symbol of the moment when a battery of unconventional baby boomers turned eastward—and inward—in such large numbers that the process became irreversible." The Integral Yoga Institute he and Peter Max founded in New York City has grown into Integral Yoga® International, the largest global Yoga organization, with centers on six continents.

The Woodstock Opening Remarks

My Beloved Sisters and Brothers:

I am very much overwhelmed with joy to see the entire youth of America gathered here in the name of the fine art of music. In fact, through the music, we can work wonders. Music is the celestial sound and it is the sound that controls the whole universe, and not the atomic vibrations. Sound energy, sound power, is much, much greater than any other powers in this world. And, one thing I would very much wish you all to remember: with sound we can make, and at the same time, break. Even in the war-field, to make the tender heart an animal, sound is used. Without that war band, that terrific sound, man will not become animal to kill his own brethren. So, that proves that we can break with sound, and if we care, we can make also.

So I am very happy to see that we are all here gathered to create some making sounds—to find that peace and joy through the celestial music. And, I am really very much honored for having [been] given this opportunity of opening this great, great music festival. I should have come a little earlier to do that job, but as you all know, still thousands of brothers and sisters are on the way and it's not that easy to reach you.

America leads the whole world in several ways. Very recently when I was in the East, the grandson of Mahatma Gandhi met me and asked me, "What's happening in America?," and I said, "America is becoming a whole. America is helping everybody in the material field, but the time has come for America to help the whole world with spirituality also." [*Audience clapping*] And, that's why from the length and breadth, we see people—thousands and thousands of people, Yoga-minded, spiritual-minded. The whole of last month I was in Hawaii and the West Coast and witnessed it again.

So, let all our actions, and all our arts, express Yoga. Through the sacred art of music, let us find peace that will pervade all over the globe. Often we hear groups of people shouting that we are going to "fight for peace." I still do not understand how they are going to fight and then find peace. [*Applause*] Therefore, let us not fight for peace, but let us find peace within ourselves first. [*Applause*] And the future of the whole world is in your hands. You can make or break. But, you are ready here to make the world and not to break it. I am seeing this. There is a dynamic manpower here. The hearts are meeting.

Just yesterday I was in Princeton, Stony Brook, in a monastery, where about 200 to 300 Catholic monks and nuns met and they asked me to talk to them under the heading of "East and West—One Heart." Here, I really wonder whether I am in the East or West. [*Applause*] If these pictures or the films are going to be shown in India, they would certainly never believe that this is taken in America. [*Applause*]

So here, the East has come into the West. And, I, with all my heart, wish a great, great success in this music festival to pave [the] way for many more festivals in many other parts of this country.

But the entire success is in your hands, not in the hands of a few organizers. Naturally, they have come forward to do some job. I met them. I admire them. But still, in your hands, the success lies. The entire world is going to watch this. The entire world is going to know what the American youth can do to the humanity. So, every one of you should be responsible for the success of this festival. [*Applause*]

And before I conclude my talk, I would like you all to join me and our group here in repeating a very simple chant. As I was reminding you of the sound power, there are certain mystical sounds which the Sanskrit terminology says as the *bijakshara*, or the "seed words." We are going to use three seed words, or the mystic words, to formulate the chant. And if you all join wholeheartedly, after the chant we are going to observe at least one whole minute of absolute silence. Not even the cameras will click at that time. And in that silent period, that one minute of silence, you are going to feel the great, great power of that sound and the wonderful peace that it can bring in you and into the whole world.

Let us have a sample of that now. The words will be: "*Hari*" is one word. "*Om*" is another word. The first chant will have these two words, "*Hari Om, Hari Om, Hari Hari Hari Om.*" The second line will be "*Hari Om, Hari Om, Hari Hari Om.*"

There will be another chant afterwards: just one word, "*Ram.*" We'll be repeating: "*Rama Rama Rama Rama Rama Rama Rama Ram.*" It's a sample. It's very easy to follow by everybody and we'll have a gentle clapping also. So, now we'll begin in a slow rhythm and gradually build it up.

Now I will request all of my friends to join me. We will repeat the line once, then allow you to follow. [The entire festival then chanted the "*Hari Om*" chant together. As time was running short, Swamiji closed instead of "*Rama*" chanting with a short "*Om Shanti*" chant.]

Thank you all very much. And once again let me express my sincere wish and prayers for the success and peace of this celebration. Thank you once again. [*Applause*]

Swami Satchidananda Reflects on His Woodstock Experience

A year prior to his passing in 2002, Swami Satchidananda was asked to speak about his memories from opening the Woodstock Festival:

Oh, now I'm supposed to talk about Woodstock?

Okay, so who were the participants of Woodstock? They were all the so-called "hippies." What made them become hippies? The false, superficial lives they were all leading. Everything was superficial, superficial, superficial.

This was a time in the 1950s, when there was intense pressure for families to live up to a certain societal model of post-war perfection and prosperity. The "Leave it to Beaver" image of what a family should be began to show cracks in it. But, it became even more important to hide these cracks. When the young people were growing up in such an atmosphere of superficiality, and hypocritical behavior, they became confused. For example, a husband and wife would be fighting like cats and dogs, but when they go out to the neighbor's home, the wife decorates herself beautifully, the husband dresses up well. He will open the door for her, "Come, honey." She will take his hand. But, it's all for show. When the dinner party is over, they come home and the husband goes one way and the wife goes in the opposite direction and they show each other the cold shoulder. Their children grew up watching all this, seeing that their parents' love was seemingly for show, for some standard that they didn't want to have imposed on them. They got fed up with that.

During the sixties, when I would put my hand on a young person's shoulder and ask, "How are you, doing?," they would immediately shed tears. I would wonder why and when I asked, I was told, "For the past eighteen years, I lived in my home. Not even once did my dad put his arm on my shoulder and ask this question. But, they gave me the car, clothes, money to spend on whatever I wanted. We had money, but I was starving for love."

When these young people went to college, what did they learn? How to make more money, how to attain more possessions, how to follow in their parents' footsteps. But, they didn't want to; they didn't feel it meant anything to them. When they would go to church, they were told, "Go to confession. Confess your sins."

So they were not interested in going to church. Home, no love; colleges teaching things of no interest; churches making you a sinner. They began to rebel against their parents, the society, the constrictions they were feeling. They didn't want to conform anymore so some dropped out, some ran away from home. They went to Haight Ashbury, some built small teepees and said, "We just want some peace, we want to find some peace." So, the life at that time made them into hippies.

Of course, as was the trend of American life at that time, everyone wanted everything quickly, instantly. They created instant coffee, instant tea, and so why not instant peace? To give that instant peace, a great "guru" arrived by the name of Timothy Leary.

Leary started supplying LSD to people. When he met me, he wanted me to join him. He said, "Well, back in those days you would go to the Himalayas, live for ten or twelve years in a cave and look for peace. Who will wait that long, when there's an instant, way of doing the same thing. See, take this pill, put it in the mouth, you enjoy peace."

So I said, "That's a good idea. We have been told that for years and years you have to sit, meditate, and pray to find the peace. But you say you can get the peace by this pill. Since you have so much success with something that takes so long, why not apply the same approach to things that take a shorter time. Since it takes at least seven years to become a doctor, engineer, or lawyer, why can't you make some engineer-making pill, lawyer-making pill? You then comfortably can close all these universities." "Swami, you are a clever man. I can't talk to you. I better say goodbye now." So, he left.

So those were the kids who gathered in the name of Woodstock. Some of the so-called refined people who were also involved in my work in the beginning, when they saw all these hippies with their flowers, bells, beads, and torn up clothes, they didn't want to move with them. They gave me a sort of challenge: "If you want us, they should leave. If they are going to be with you, we will go away. They smell, they are like pigs."

The so-called refined people called the hippies "pigs." So, I told them, they may be pigs to you, but they are my kids. I didn't ask them to come to me and I can't ask them to go away. If you don't feel comfortable, you can leave me and go. And some of them left.

I was working with the so-called hippie pigs, and one day, a call came asking me to come to Woodstock, because they were worried. They explained they were having a big gathering in the name of peace and music. The symbol of the festival was a white dove sitting on the handle of the guitar. Peace and music. They said to me, "You have to come and say something to us." At the same time, some of the people who had heard about this gathering begged me not to go. I asked them why? They explained, "There's going to be a big turmoil there. All the restless people will be gathering there."

I said, "Well, God seems to be wanting me there. Let me go. So by the time I went there to Woodstock, it was full for 30-40 miles all around. All the roads were blocked because there was so much traffic. No cars could even move down the road, so people drove as far as they could go and they would get out of the cars and leave them and walk.

So all the roads were blocked by cars. Thirty miles away, our car stopped; I couldn't go further. Luckily, we saw a police helicopter flying. So we lit a torch to attract the police, And seeing the flame, the police helicopter landed there. They asked us what was happening. Luckily, someone who came with me, said, "Swamiji is supposed to go, and open the Woodstock Festival. We got held up here and couldn't go any further. Can you take him there?" They accepted and they put me in the helicopter, took me there, and dropped me near the stage.

That's how I entered into the festival. I found out that the organizers were scared. They thought there would be about thirty- to forty-thousand people. But hundreds of thousands of people came! Seeing the crowd, they got frightened. Then Peter Max and a few others who knew me told them, "It's better to get the Swami here. Let him come and say something nice and open the festival.

That's how they invited me. And, I felt, I have to go there. When I arrived on the stage, it was like an ocean of human heads all over the hill. I didn't know what to tell them. So as I usually do, I went there, sat there, and looked at them. Then, something came to me. I just talked to them. I told them it was a great gathering and nothing like that had ever happened anywhere, or at least in America. I explained that I had seen that their sign was the peace symbol and the festival was about peace and music. That's when I told them to remember that they had gathered there in the name of music and peace—nothing else.

I briefly mentioned that I had recently met the grandson of Mahatma Gandhi. He had come to a conference on moral rearmament in Sri Lanka, then Ceylon. I was there at that time with a group of thirty to forty American hippies.

Gandhiji's grandson saw these young people, and he said to me, "They seem to be all young people and I hear you traveled all over India and then came over here. I would like to know what they feel about India and the Indian youth their age." So I replied, "Why don't you ask them directly?"

One woman got up and said, "Mr. Gandhi, we're very disappointed. Having heard about India and its philosophy, having been studying Yoga ourselves, we thought it would be such a beautiful place that when we landed in Bombay we knelt on the ground and prayed, and worshipped this holy land. But when we met some of the youth, and we asked them about Yoga, *pranayama*, *Bhagavad Gita*, and so on, they didn't seem to know anything about any of it. They were looking at us as sort of crazy people because we were asking all these kinds of questions. And, on the other hand, their interest was in our cameras, our jeans, in our watches and radios. They asked 'Did you declare these in the customs? If not, can you sell them to us?' They knew nothing about Yoga."

Mr. Gandhi was a little disappointed. He looked at me and asked, "Is that true?" I told him, "Well, that is true. Because we completely ignore the children and we haven't taught them anything about Yoga and their spiritual heritage. If we leave it like this, in a few years if our children want to know about Yoga, they will have to wait for the American youth to come and teach them." And it exactly happened that way. After a few years, when I went with another group of people, they wanted me to leave one or two Americans to teach them Yoga.

That was the situation at that time. So, I explained to those at the festival that the world had a big hope in them and I asked them to please not disappoint them. Let there be peace only and music only. I suggested that we all do some peace chanting.

Later, I was on television on the "Mike Douglas Show" with Peter Max. Mike asked me the question, "How do you feel about Woodstock?" I said, "I feel fine. But what did you people—the media—talk about?

You only reported that people were taking drugs, people were going naked, there was trash everywhere. You failed to notice that all the 500,000 people stayed together happily without any police, without any problems. You didn't appreciate all the good things." He apologized and said, "Unfortunately, if we write nice things, nobody reads it."

Oh, boy, I still remember the sound of the crowd. It still vibrates in my ears. All those 500,000 people chanting, "*Hari Om, Hari Om, Hari, Hari, Hari Om!*" The whole sky was filled with that sound. And luckily, for three days, day and night, the music was going on and even amidst the rain and lack of shelter, it all went beautifully.

Life Lessons from the Woodstock Guru

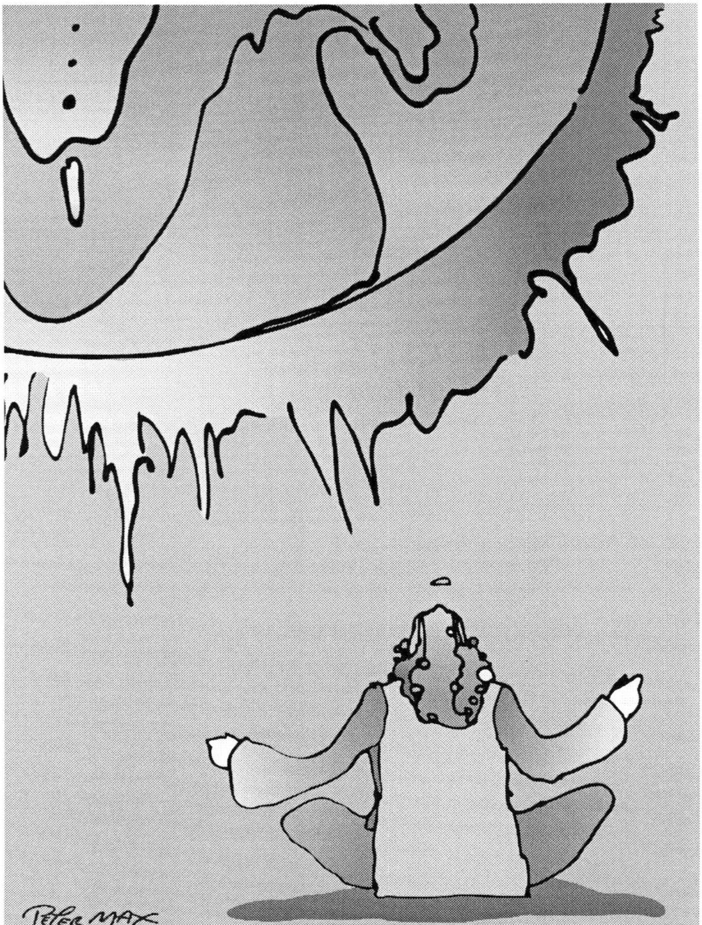

The year 2019 marked the 50th anniversary of the Woodstock Music Festival and Swami Satchidananda's opening remarks and prayer, which set the tone for a historic three days of peace and music that the world came to know and remember as Woodstock.

The values of Woodstock—peace, love, harmony—are as important today as they were 50 years ago, yet they have gotten lost in the cacophony of a society that may be in as much turmoil today as it was then.

Swami Satchidananda's message focused on uniting body, mind, and spirit in a state of equanimity through Yoga and leading a selfless life in service to others as a pathway to peace, harmony, and love.

His teachings offer guidance on how to achieve this connection, specifically:

Find Your Inner Ease

Swami Satchidananda recommended finding the ease that each of us is born and to recognize that disease is essentially dis-ease: disturbed ease. We can utilize the ancient Yoga practices and the power of the mind to find the disturbance and remove it and to take care not to disturb our ease, once restored.

"Actually you don't have to do anything to heal the body and mind. If you don't interfere, the body and mind heals itself. There is a healer within everyone. We don't have to do anything to put health into the body. We have to stop doing the negative things that disturb the body and mind and then the good happens by itself." —Swami Satchidananda

See the Same Spirit in Others as We See in Ourselves

Swami Satchidananda was an interfaith pioneer. He believed in a universal spiritual vision—not that there should be one world religion, but rather that we appreciate the diversity of faiths, while realizing what unites us all: we are one human and spiritual family. When we identify with our physical bodies and our minds, we see the differences that make us feel separate from one another rather than experiencing the Spirit that unites us. Once we realize that behind these superficial differences there is something that unites us all, we can then realize that everyone else is equally a spark of the same divinity.

"If we want to be happy, we should work for the happiness of all people everywhere. In order to have a better world, a more peaceful world, we must have a

universal approach. It's time to know each other and to live as one global family. With that kind of feeling the whole world will be a haven and a heaven."
—Swami Satchidananda

Seek Inner Peace and Joy

Swami Satchidananda taught that if our spiritual goal is to realize our true nature, this will lead to an awareness of our inner peace, happiness, and joy. Usually the mind is not calm and peaceful because there are constantly waves across its surface—caused by desires we are running after, happiness we're seeking in other people or material things. If we realize that this will only lead to more disturbance in the mind, we can choose more positive thoughts that will not disturb the mind. By letting go of attachments and self-centered thoughts, replacing them with more selflessness we maintain our tranquility.

"Happiness does not come from outside you. No one ever gives you happiness, but only reflects your own inner happiness. You have the strength, courage, and capacity to experience the peace and joy within and to share it with everyone. If you want to be happy, work for the happiness of all people everywhere."
—Swami Satchidananda

The Legacy of Woodstock and the Woodstock Guru

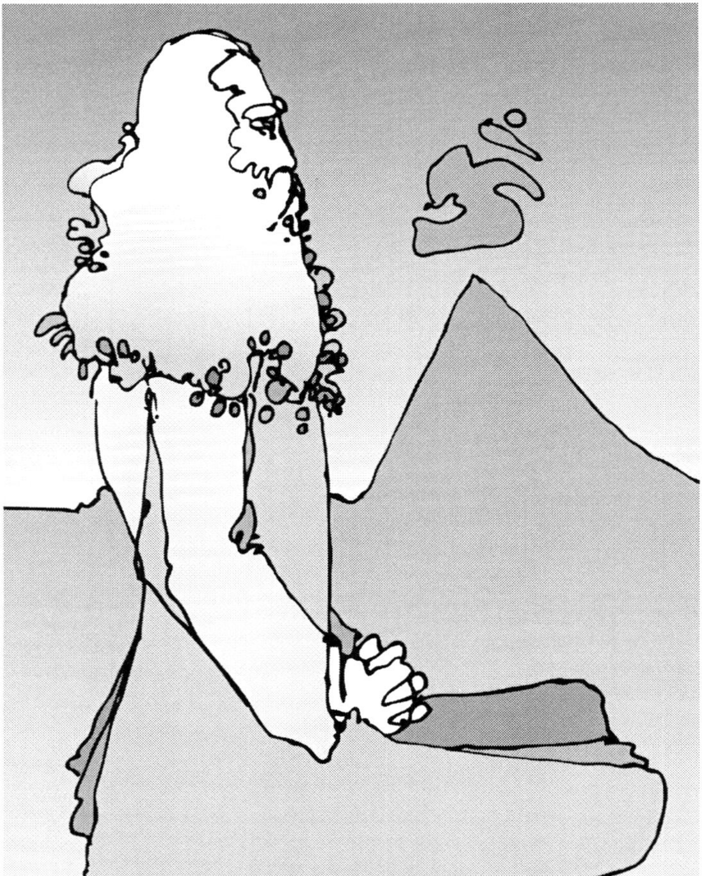

His words of peace, love, and harmony remain the legacy of the Woodstock generation and those who are continuing to birth the modern Yoga, wellness, and personal transformation movement. Swami Satchidananda left his body in 2002, yet his spirit lives on through Integral Yoga, Yogaville, and all who embrace and share his message.

In Honor of Woodstock 50:
50 Inspiring Quotes by Swami Satchidananda

1. **The human body is a temple, keep it strong and supple.**

   You can make every act of yours holy. Feel that your body is a divine temple, and that God is dwelling within you. When you eat something, feel it is the divine within you that is accepting it, so you are eating for the sake of God. When you bathe yourself, feel that you are cleaning the temple of God. When you put some unwanted thing in you, think, *I am polluting the temple of God, so I should not do that*. Even if you think something bad, you will feel: *Oh, the God within is watching me, how can I be thinking like this*? By continuously keeping the mind on God in this way, every action becomes holy.

2. **Love for the sake of love, because loving makes you happy.**

Love everyone and everything. By loving everything, you are really loving yourself. Everything is nothing but the expression of yourself. If you stand in front of a mirror, you love that reflection. You smile at it and it smiles at you. In the same way, the whole world is your projection. You love because you are made of love, because loving makes you happy; not because you have to love. The scriptures say to love your neighbor as yourself. That means you have to see your Self in the other person. Real love is possible only when you see everything as your own expression. When we go beyond the name and form, you will find that the essence is the same.

3. **The sun is always shining whether the clouds are there or not.**

It is the nature of the mind to constantly change. You should learn how to surf on the waves of the mind, rather than being tossed and beaten by them. Always affirm that you are not going to be the slave of the mind; you are going to be the master.

Exercise your mastery. If something terrible comes, you think, *I can't stand it another minute*. But if you just hold on a little longer, it passes. Sometimes black clouds come, but the sun is always shining behind them. Don't give up. If you give up and run somewhere else, there will be a difficult situation to face there too. Wherever you go, your own mind goes with you.

4. **To have maximum and endless joy learn to be non-attached.**

How can you maintain your happiness and joy always? Ask yourself why you are unhappy. Every time you are unhappy over something, the first thing to do is to analyze the cause. You will always find there is attachment in some area. If you don't want to be unhappy, you will come to the conclusion, *Oh, I should not be attached to that. When I am attached, I feel unhappy*. You may ask, "But what about people?" You can be friendly, you can love them, but you should not be attached to them. There is a difference between attachment and love. Love means that you think of others and put their benefit first. Attachment means thinking of your benefit first.

5. **The entire nature is ready to guide you, if you really look for guidance.**

Nothing happens without a reason. The reason is to teach you some lesson. There's always a good lesson in whatever happens to you, even in the midst of your losses. I don't mean only in material losses; it's that way even with losses of your near and dear. You can get back on the right track; get up and walk. If you don't feel strong enough, you can ask for guidance. The whole world is a university, and we are all here learning. Every individual should think, *I am the only student. Everyone and everything are my professors.* All others are simply helping to educate you, to pass through each level. You should learn to understand and accept that.

6. **Nothing is impossible for a one-pointed mind.**

When the mind is concentrated, it gains more strength. If you gather all the thought forms and concentrate on one idea or object, the mind will reveal the inner secret of that idea. That's what inventors do. They are deeply concentrated, their minds are one-pointed, so nature reveals its secrets to them. Because these individuals' minds were one-pointed, they could penetrate the secret of the atom. That control is possible. Slowly train the mind in such a way that it is always under your control, and, whenever you want, you will be able to make it still. With that you can gain anything you want in this world. There is nothing in this world that a one-pointed mind cannot gain.

7. **An action becomes perfect when it brings some benefit to someone and no harm to anyone.**

Yoga is perfection in action. If the result of that action brings benefit to all people concerned—to the person who does that action and to the person who enjoys the benefit of it, without bringing harm to anybody—then it's a yogic action. If it's going to bring harm even to one person, or if it's going to build up tension in your own mind, it's not yogic. When you do something and expect a reward as a result of that action, then, even before you start doing it, you build up tension. Instead, if the mind is kept free from any expectation whatsoever and if your action is done just for the sake of others, then that action is yogic.

8. **Let total love, universal love, emanate from within.**

The more you think of your problems the deeper you'll go into them. It's as if you are meditating on them, which is like pouring gasoline onto a fire. If you pour love on hate, that's like pouring water onto fire. Put in new, constructive ideas, and let those ideas take the place of the mental fixations. That's the spiritual way, the yogic approach. If you hate somebody, instead of trying to find ways to get out of that hatred, just ignore it and try to love. Think of love, love, love and the hatred will go away, automatically. With regular practice of both physical and mental Yoga, you can easily overcome challenges in life, instead of worrying about them and constantly thinking about them.

9. **If you are content your daily needs will be met.**

In Yoga, all that we want is a balanced and contented mind; it's not how much you have that is going to make you happy. The more you run after things, the more they go away. If you are contented, things come to you by themselves, even if you don't want them. Have a trial week without wanting. Stop wanting anything. See how many things come to you. Because everything and everybody likes to be with a contented person. If you are happy, everything comes. You should bring out the fragrance of happiness. When there is nice fragrance, when there is honey in you, you don't have to advertise for the bees to come to you. They just come.

10. If there is heaven in your mind, you see heaven everywhere.

One brother says, "Whenever I come back to my home, I feel that I am in heaven." If you ask another brother, he may say the opposite: "Whenever I come home, I feel I am in hell." Why should the same house seem like hell and heaven to two different people? It's in their thoughts and attitudes. According to their mind and their approach to the world, things seem good or bad. There's nothing good or bad outside, it's according to your approach that you see the world the way you do. When I say approach, I mean according to the coloring of our minds. If you can keep control over the mind, wherever you are will be a heaven.

11. **Be married to your peace and joy.**

Relationships need not be difficult. If you don't have any selfish purpose, then you don't expect anything and you don't lose anything. You aren't attached to that relationship. Realize that you don't have to have a relationship to be happy. You are already married to your peace and joy. But you don't appreciate that. That means you don't realize your own true nature, which is happiness. The minute you realize that you are always happy, that you are always peaceful whether you have a relationship or not, that you have a permanent relationship within, then you no longer worry about an outside relationship. If it comes, fine, if it doesn't come, wonderful. You don't depend on anything or anyone for your happiness.

12. **Every failure is a stepping stone for your future success.**

Making mistakes is part of learning so, when you make a mistake, don't get upset. Learn from your mistakes, and then don't repeat them. You are free to make another kind of mistake, but not the same mistake. Every mistake, every failure is a stepping stone for future success. You have to fail. Look at Olympic champions, great runners. Did they run out of the womb at birth? They couldn't even move their bodies much. How long did it take for those future champions to be able to stand? How many times did they fall? That is the process of learning. Don't be afraid of falling. Let every failure help you to learn a little better for your future success.

13. Have an easeful body, peaceful mind and a useful life.

Keep yourself healthy, happy and thus holy. Or, in other words, be easeful physically, be peaceful mentally and then be useful in your life. And to accomplish this all you have to do is just to be vigilant constantly and to stay away, to renounce, to reject whatever it is that would come in the way and disturb your ease of the body, peace of the mind. It's not that you're going to acquire that ease and peace newly. It is there already. If you could only take good care of it and see that you don't disturb it, it remains. When you're easeful and peaceful, then you can be useful. Otherwise, you may even harm rather than help the situation.

14. We are all one.

Yoga means to unite, to come together. The moment we think of coming together we really become yogis, so let our entire lives be based on this coming together, being together, becoming together. We should realize that oneness that is already within us. We are already one, but, unfortunately, nobody has ever answered exactly why we are separate. Different saints have explained the cause of separation in many ways: It is due to ignorance, to illusion or to life in the material world. There are many answers to why we feel separate from each other, but, probably, the true answer will come to us only after we realize our oneness. In that oneness, you find peace within and without.

15. Think you are happy and you are happy.

Think well, you will be well. Think ill, you'll be ill. Think happy, you will be happy. As you think, so you become. It's all your thought. Sometimes you might not be thinking ill of yourself, but you are thinking ill of others. Whether it is about you or somebody else, that is what you are thinking. When you think of that, you will become that and you will be hurting yourself. You can meditate on a monkey. What will you become? Monkey. So, even to practice Yoga, you should know what to think in order to make yourself comfortable and happy. Throughout your life, you should always think well. Train your eyes to see the bright side of everything.

16. All you have to do is be.

To enjoy life to the fullest, just be. If something comes, let it come. If it goes, let it go. Enjoy the coming. Enjoy the going. The only way to enjoy is to just be what you are. You're not going to enjoy by getting things. If you are going to enjoy by getting things, you are going to be depressed by losing things. True joy doesn't come from anywhere. Nothing brings you joy. No person brings you joy. You yourself are joyful always. So enjoy that. Depend on nothing, because nothing from outside can make you joyful. Just be good and do good. Then God will be happy with you, and you'll find real peace and joy in your life.

17. **Everything on this earth has a purpose.**

God has a purpose for you. If the purpose is over, not even an ounce of breath will be wasted on you. So the fact that you are still alive means that God wants you to live, to do some of God's work. Everything on this earth has a purpose and that purpose is to be useful and bring some benefit to somebody. It is for that purpose that you are eating; it is for that purpose you are breathing. When you go to sleep, think: *By sleeping, I will be rested enough to get up early in the morning to serve others.* Living this way, your mind is always free from all kinds of anxieties, worries, fears and hatred.

18. **Don't ever, ever put yourself down.**

Self-judgment and negativity will affect your heart, your mind and your personality. Analyze: *Is it helpful for me to have these negative thoughts? Is it constructive or destructive? I become what I think. If my thoughts are like this, what will I become*? When you realize that, you won't want to do it anymore. That's why, at least for your own sake, if not for the sake of others, you shouldn't develop any negative thoughts about yourself or about anybody else. No one interested in his or her own welfare, physical and mental, should invite negative thoughts. Begin to love yourself. Find love within yourself. Because everything begins at home. If you have love, you can give love to others.

19. It's all for fun. Just watch and enjoy the show.

Jivanmuktas are souls liberated from the bondage of the mind. To those souls, everything is fun, everything is a show, nothing is a surprise. The nature of the mind is to be restless. The mind is like a screen—it reflects all kinds of images. When you go to a cinema, you see many kinds of shows: good, bad, violent, silly. You watch everything. It's fun. The same way, you should watch your own mind putting on a show and have fun watching it. Sometimes you might forget this and take the life seriously. You have to step back from the mind and watch it. Be the witness always and you will have fun and always enjoy the show.

20. No one ever gives you happiness, but only reflects your own inner happiness.

Ultimately, we're all looking for happiness. But

it's not something that has to be brought in from outside. Happiness is already within you, and is to be experienced. No one can bring you happiness, they only reflect your own inner happiness. If you want to experience the joy within, liberate yourself from your own self-made bondage. Nobody on earth is interested in binding you. Even if someone were interested, nobody could do that. It's completely in your hands to be bound or to be free. If you think that you are bound, you are bound. If you think that you are free right this moment, and that from time immemorial you have never been bound, then you are free.

21. Accomplishing small things will improve your self-confidence.

You know what's wrong but maybe you don't have the willpower to stay away from that. How can you develop the will? By discipline and regular practice. You develop that by doing little things. Don't start with a big job that you can't easily do; if you fail, you'll lose confidence. Accomplishing small things will improve your self-confidence. Then one day, even the biggest thing will be the easiest for you. Will means application and training of the mind. Making the mind work in a positive way. It's achieved slowly. It's easy to say, "Oh, I'm not made for that. It's too much for me. Not everyone can do that." Such excuses are self-delusion. Without will, we cannot achieve anything.

22. Find the peace within first and then express it.

Yoga believes in transforming the individual even before it thinks of the world. Perhaps you are thinking: *Oh, I must transform the world. I must find peace in the world.* In finding the peace, you lose your peace. How many people fight in the name of peace? By fighting they disturb the little peace that is already there. You can't bring peace to others unless you first have peace yourself. So, if you are really interested in helping the world, find peace within yourself. Then you are really contributing something to the world, so that it can find it's own peace. Otherwise you will just be talking and talking about peace. By transforming yourself, you transform your part of the world.

23. The greatest victory you can win is the victory over your own mind.

You don't have to be a slave to your body, mind and senses. The Yoga practices enable you to develop the willpower to resist the whims and fancies of the lower mind. Somebody said that the greatest victory in the entire world is not by winning wars and other things. The greatest victory is the victory over your own mind. So work toward that. It may take some time, but perseverance brings perfection. And remember Patanjali's words: "Practice becomes well-grounded when done for a long time, without break and with great interest." With zeal, one can achieve anything one wants. Nothing is impossible. The mind is a fantastic machine. It has the capability of achieving anything it wants.

24. Do your best and leave the rest.

Let us just do our duty and leave the rest to nature. Let whatever you do be for the benefit of others. If you can, do something. If you cannot, accept it. Somebody else will do it; it's not that you have to do it all yourself. You didn't create the world and you're not going to save it. Honestly try to do your part, but know that you aren't the end-all. If a thing is meant to happen, it will happen. Start it and if it has to happen through you, more energy will come to you. If not, you will very soon know that you are not to do that. Accept it. Do your best, and leave the rest.

25. True love knows no bargains. It is one-way traffic, giving, giving, giving.

Just let your nature be giving and loving. That's divine love, an outpouring with no expectation for anything back. Love knows no bargain, it only gives and gives and gives. That's what is called universal love. If you love just for the joy of loving, it won't fall away. You can love anybody and everybody with that pure love. But if you love only waiting for some love in return, in time you will surely be disappointed. Learn to love without trying to always make some kind of bargain out of it. Learn to love all humanity, nature, animals and plants. Then you won't have to do anything. Just by being yourself you will be loving and serving one and all.

26. Who will be the happiest person? The one who brings happiness to others.

What is the sign of a healthy person? You are relaxed everywhere—always at ease and in peace, within and without. A healthy person hates no one, dislikes nothing. Total love, universal love emanates from within. There is no tension anywhere, no stress or friction. These are the signs of real health. A person who is healthy doesn't hurt anyone. Not only are you unafraid, but you see that others are not afraid of you. The "others" include animals, plants, everything. A healthy person emits always and only a loving and pure vibration. Who will be the happiest person? The one who brings happiness to others. That means our minds should be well-balanced under all conditions. That is Yoga.

27. Obstacles draw out our inner capabilities.

The world has been created for you to make use of and to grow. You can't run away. You will face the same problems wherever you go. Even if you're running, you're not escaping. The same kind of challenge will come there also, in a little different form. Why? Because difficulties come to make us strong. Wherever we go in the cosmos, we're going to be cooked by our experiences. So we should accept this until we are roasted well. Life is an obstacle race, and a challenge has been presented to you. Giving up is easy. Instead, try to face any challenge with all your heart and strength. You can't run away. Find the ways and means to do it.

28. In the universal plan, we're all just doing our part.

Every job is equally important. There's no superior or inferior work. You can perform any work with joy if you know that every job is equally good. You lose the joy of doing things when you don't understand the importance of them, when you compare your work with someone else's work. There's no blue collar work or white collar work. If you want to see it that way, your legs are doing blue collar work. Your head is doing white collar work. Your blue collar workers have to take the white collar worker wherever it wants to go. We are the ones who create all this superiority/inferiority. The world needs everything. Every action is equally good. Do your part with joy.

29. **Faith and fear do not go together.**

Fear isn't going to help you in any way. Fear makes the mind lose all its strength. Remember, even to have fear, you must have faith in your fear. You have faith in your fear, and that's why you are afraid. But you should know that fear isn't going to bring you any benefit. Faith and fear don't go together. Either you have faith, or you have fear. You know that you're alive now. Why don't you enjoy the now, rather than worry about the future? Enjoy both getting and losing. So, if you know the ultimate truth, there's no reason to fear. Don't let that fear come near you at any time. Learn to live in the golden present.

30. **Keep harmony in your house as your top priority.**

Real spiritual experience brings harmony. What's the use of those other experiences if you can't live comfortably, harmoniously, lovingly with ten people? Everybody should love you. To me that's what you call spiritual experience. Keep that in mind: *I will live a life that will make everybody love me. Nobody should look at me with even a little dismay.* Only if you can do that, are you growing spiritually. Prove you're becoming a beautiful person. Don't argue; instead, let your family see that you are being helped by what you are doing. Prove the benefit of your practice by your own example. As a spiritual person, you should see that there is harmony present in the family in all situations.

31. Take it easy, but don't be lazy.

As far as possible, live simply and lead a natural life. Don't tax your brain, don't tax your mind and don't tax your system by overloading and overstressing. Take it easy, but not lazy. Yoga is something very easy, quite enjoyable. If anybody says, "Oh, I am trying hard to become a yogi," I say that person will never become a yogi. One can never become a yogi by trying hard; that is the exact opposite of Yoga. Yoga should be a joyful celebration. It's very important to find the golden medium. Use your common sense. There's no hard-and-fast rule about these things. If there is one common rule for all practices, it's this: go to your capacity, but never overdo.

32. **Know your own strength and avoid disturbances to your peace of mind.**

If you lose your peace, you won't be able to help anyone else, let alone yourself. A spiritual seeker is like a tender young tree that needs a fence to protect it while it's growing. It's easily disturbed and affected. If the farmer removes the fence, the cattle will come and chew the plant up After it has grown, it becomes a strong tree, offering fruits and shade for all and nothing can disturb it. As a young plant, you need discipline for your own protection; as a grown tree, you are free to protect others. Know your own strength now and avoid disturbances. Choose your company wisely. After all, what is the most precious thing? Peace of mind.

33. **The simple way to always be happy is to accept everything.**

Pleasure, accept it. Pain, accept it. Profit, accept it. Loss, accept it. By accepting everything, the great benefit is: You don't disturb your peace. You are always happy. That's what real Yoga is. That is what real spiritual attainment is. That's what you call enlightenment. So, learn to accept things. That doesn't mean that you shouldn't think of doing something, wanting to get something. It's better not to have any wants, but if you still want it, okay. Have your wants under one condition: the wants should be approved by the Higher Power. If you get it, all right, it was approved. If you don't get it, all right, it was disapproved. There's no harm in that kind of want.

34. You are never alone; God is nearer than your own heart.

Long ago I used to feel lonely until I realized that there's a Beloved who is always in me, with me, next to me, closer than my heart. Since then, I have found that I'm never alone. If you depend on anything or anybody outside you to be a companion, it's impossible to have that companion always with you. Even if another person wants to be with you always, he or she cannot. Your own spirit, your own Self or the God within you is always there. The moment you realize that, you will never feel lonely. The outside company is fine, but don't depend on it. Be independent of everything. If it comes, fine. If it goes, wonderful.

35. The more you give, the more you get. That's nature's law.

If you are a good channel, you won't keep anything for yourself except what you need, and you will pass along the rest. Then more things will come to you. It's like a fountain that you have drawn forth. The more you draw, the more it comes. You never feel the want. Sometimes you will get so much that you will be tired of giving. But at no point should you try to stop it from flowing through you. If you stop the flow, you'll notice that it gets stagnant. And, if you try to imprison anything or cling to it, it will hesitate to come. Things love to move freely. So let everything flow to you and through you.

36. You are not the body, not the mind. You are the knower.

Imagine, you say, "My mind is totally upset today. Yesterday I was all peaceful, happy. Today, I am disturbed." What's the common thing behind these statements? The common factor is that you know. You know that you're disturbed; you know you're not disturbed. The true you is that which knows everything, while the superficial you, is the mind. Although your mind is disturbed in some way today, the knower of your mind is not disturbed. Your mind was happy yesterday, and now, today, your mind is not happy. You might say, "I am my body, my mind, my intelligence, my ego." Of course you seem to have those things. But, who are you in reality? You are the knower.

37. There is always a positive way of looking at things.

Think in a positive way. Bring out the good qualities, the positive side in you and the negative will get cured by itself. Convince your conscious mind, and let the conviction sink into the subconscious mind. You can even make a recording of your own and play it while you sleep. It will slowly sink into your subconscious mind. Negative thoughts have gone into the subconscious, and you need to replace them with positive thoughts. Put reminders everywhere until the negativity is completely rooted out. The yogic way is to put a new, opposite thought into the mind so that the undesirable thought will be squeezed out. And if you can't do it all by yourself, get help from others.

38. **Ask advice from your own pure Self.**

Your conscience is the part of the divine in you, the Guru within. Ask advice from your pure Self. It's not necessary always to get advice from someone outside. The conscience is constantly giving us advice, but sometimes you don't listen to it. You may not even want to listen. Someone else can only help you for a while. You should learn to ask that buddy within. Sometimes you might feel a conflict: *I don't know which is the Self and which is the ego.* Ultimately, you have to develop the capacity to discriminate within yourself. That's why meditation is so important. Until you become established in that, at least in meditation you should be able to hear your own inner Self.

39. **Keep up your physical and mental purity so that you can recognize your inner light.**

Eat clean food—the food that would come to you with loving vibrations. See the proper sights, hear the proper sounds and think the proper ideas. Everything that goes into you is your food. Food for the mind, food for the eyes, food for the ears, food for the nose. Let those foods always be clean and not disturb your ease. Build the nerves with *pranayama*, and build love with chants, psalms, or mantras. You can use Yoga practices to smooth any hectic day. When you get up, you should perform your spiritual practices. Begin each day with the words of a great saint or prophet. Before you practice, pray for help; use your mantra and have faith in your teacher.

40. The only requirement to see your true Self is a clean, peaceful mind.

The goal of human life is to know the Self and experience eternal happiness and supreme peace. All the great sages who have realized this peace and joy have told us that the moment you keep your mind calm and serene, you can enjoy supreme happiness. A restless mind is an impure mind; an impure mind is a restless mind. If you could keep the mind clean, it will find its calmness. The mind is nothing but a bunch of thoughts. When the thoughts are clean, the mind is clean. When the thoughts are ugly with jealousy, selfishness, hatred or vengeance, it's a dirty mind that thinks and becomes those thoughts. So take care to keep the mind clean.

41. The cause of your suffering is your wrong approach to things.

When you understand the ups and downs of the world in the proper way, you'll see that it's up to you to understand this and raise above it all. Then, you can ride over the waves with skill. You'll say, "Oh, these waves are the nature of the world; they won't defeat me." That's the knowledge you want. Then, you won't get upset over anything. Sometimes you may think that someone else is making you suffer, or that not getting what you wanted is making you miserable or only by acquiring things will you be happy. No. Suffering is self-made. Nobody can make you suffer. It's your own attitude, your own ignorance. Sorrow is nothing but what you borrow.

42. You are your own friend and your own enemy.

The same mind can be a friend or an enemy. You should analyze it: *Will this vision, desire or experience help me, or cause trouble*? Use your own intelligence. If the experience is likely to cause problems, then it's a trick of the mind. Ignore it. But if the mind brings you something useful, take it. One part of the mind is always *sattvic* (balanced). That part always talks to the other parts saying, *Why do you keep swinging back and forth between restlessness and dullness?* The *sattvic* part doesn't swing at all. It's always calm. Even if your life appears sometimes to be swinging, know that you're always united with the peaceful Self which isn't affected by the swinging.

43. Stay away from anything that disturbs your peace of mind.

When something or someone wants to come to you, question yourself: *By keeping it around me, will I lose my peace?* If you think that, *Yes, it might disturb my peace*, then tell it: "Sorry." Always think in terms of your peace. Which will give you permanent peace and which will give you temporary peace and disturb it afterwards? Ask that for everything. That's what you call discrimination. That should be applied in everything: eating, sleeping, drinking, talking, walking, doing—everything. The pudding is very tasty. You feel like having some more. Question yourself: *Will this affect my peace*? Apply this to everything. So that means you are constantly aware of your peace. You are doing everything in terms of peace.

44. Let people see something beautiful in you. Let them see the light in you.

All I teach is that you learn to be selfless. That is Karma Yoga, selfless service. When you work for yourself, you develop anxiety, you develop worry and fear. When you work for others there is joy. If the others need your service, it's their business to take care of you. Remember: If you decide to take care of yourself, you are the only person to take care of you. If you let others take care of you, so many will do that. That's the secret. Your life can be a beautiful fruit for all humanity to enjoy. And when you shine with peace and joy, you expose to that light not only yourself, but other people as well.

45. Keep the lake of the mind always calm and clean.

Whenever your peace is disturbed, reflect and you will realize, *I wanted something, so that want fell into my calm mind, as a stone falling into a lake, and it started creating ripples.* If you try every time to adjust the mind by fulfilling its wants, there's no end. Even if you say, "Oh, this will be the last desire, the last thing I want and then no more," how many times would you have said that? You thought that by fulfilling your desires, by enjoying them, they can come to an end. It's something like adding more fuel, thinking that you can put out the fire. The more you enjoy them, the more you reconfirm and renew the desires.

46. Bear insult, bear injury. This is the greatest Yoga.

Anyone can do *asanas*, *pranayama*, meditate. That's not great Yoga. Don't think, *Oh, I can do headstand for a half an hour, hold my breath for a couple of minutes.* A fish goes underwater for a long time holding the breath. Real Yoga is: adapt, adjust, accommodate. Wherever you are, adapt yourself to that situation. Adjust yourself. Accommodate. Bear insult, bear injury. This is the greatest Yoga. That doesn't mean that I don't ask you to do *asanas* and *pranayama*. Do that. Maybe it will help you to strengthen the mind in order to bear insult and injury, because you need a strong mind, an understanding mind. The world gives you plenty of opportunities to watch, train and strengthen your mind.

47. You are already enlightened.

There's enlightenment in us all. However, it's covered over and sometimes forgotten. The light is there already. You are not given the light by anyone—not even by a spiritual teacher. You are that light. You are the image of God. Nobody has to give you enlightenment. If somebody has to give you enlightenment, then, one day, you'll lose it. You're already enlightened, but you don't know that. Your mind doesn't want to accept that. If the mind accepts that, it loses its power. The mind doesn't want to lose its power. In a way, it's a tug-of-war between you and your mind. The mind wants you to be its slave. Through Yoga, you are learning to control the mind.

48. You can become the master of your own mind.

Once, a man was riding his camel through the desert on his way to sell his wares. He was lost in his own thoughts, planning where to go, whom to see, what profit was to be made. While he was busy planning, the camel was also lost in thought: *When is this devil going to stop and give me food and water*? In the same way, you may have your plan for doing your Yoga practices regularly, but your mind may be plotting something different. If you know that, you won't be disheartened by this trick of the mind. You'll need confidence to learn to direct your mind where you want it to go in order to live a yogic life.

49. The dedicated ever enjoy supreme peace, therefore live only to serve.

The human tendency is to think, Me first. But, living a life of dedication means putting others first, and giving back more than we receive. A yogi always try to give back more than what we take from nature, and that is called yagna. When you accept something from somebody and then give the same thing back, it's just business. Suppose somebody gives you $50 and you give back the $50. That's fair business. If you don't give it, you're a thief. If you give the same amount, you're a businessperson. But nature expects you to become something greater: a dedicated person. A dedicated person will always offer more. Such a person will always be filled with peace and joy.

50. Breath is life. Let every breath bring fresh energy into your system.

You breathe, but do you know how to breathe properly? Even the little breath you do take in, isn't always taken consciously. It just happens to go in and out by divine grace. But if you become conscious of the breathing, and make it a little deeper, you can charge the whole body with fresh life. With a powerful, full breath, you can take in seven times more oxygen. That means much greater purification of the blood, as well as oxygenation of the entire body. Every cell in your body is a living being by itself. If you know how to do proper breathing, you can live long, with enough energy in your body to keep it in perfect health.

About the Woodstock Guru and Integral Yoga

"The very definition of Yoga is tranquility. Equanimity in body and mind is Yoga. Real Yoga is functioning with tranquility in the midst of activity."
—Swami Satchidananda

Sri Swami Satchidananda was one of the great Yoga masters to bring the classical Yoga tradition to the Western world in the 1960s. He taught Yoga postures and meditation, and he introduced students to a vegetarian diet and a more compassionate lifestyle.

The distinctive teachings that he brought with him blend the physical discipline of Yoga, the spiritual philosophy of India, and the interfaith ideals he pioneered. These techniques and concepts influenced a generation and spawned a Yoga culture that is flourishing today. Currently, over 35 million Americans (and 300 million worldwide) practice Yoga as a means for managing stress, promoting health, slowing down the aging process, and creating a more meaningful life.

The Integral Yoga teachings of Swami Satchidananda are a pathway to an "easeful body, peaceful mind, and a useful life," as he said, and to harmony, balance, integration, and Self-realization.

The Integral Yoga method is a synthesis of six classical branches of Yoga: Hatha, Raja, Japa, Karma, Bhakti, and Jnana. Its aim is to purify and calm the body and mind in order to experience the peace and joy that is our true nature. Integral Yoga practitioners bring that peace into the world by fostering interfaith harmony and leading service-oriented lives.

Founded in 1966, there are currently 30 Integral Yoga centers on six of the seven continents and 6,000 teachers worldwide. Today, these centers and certified Yoga teachers and Yoga therapists throughout the United States and abroad offer classes, workshops, retreats. They also offer Yoga teacher training featuring all aspects of Integral Yoga and a Yoga therapist training program.

Many Integral Yoga teachers and therapists have become leaders in the changing paradigm of modern Yoga and healthcare, as well as founding successful programs for specific populations. Integral Yoga-inspired programs include Dr. Dean Ornish's landmark work in reversing heart disease, Dr. Michael Lerner's noted Commonweal Cancer Help program, Sonia Sumar's Yoga for the Special Child, and Rev. Jivana Heyman's Accessible Yoga, among many others.

In 1979, Swami Satchidananda was inspired to establish Satchidananda Ashram–Yogaville. Founded on his teachings, it is a large residential community, with a programs and retreat center, training academy for Yoga and Yoga therapy. It is a haven where people can study and practice the teachings of Swami Satchidananda and Integral Yoga. It is a multifaith community where people of various backgrounds can come together to realize their essential oneness.

One of the focal points of Yogaville is the Light Of Truth Universal Shrine (LOTUS). This unique interfaith shrine honors the Spirit that unites all the world religions, while it celebrates their diversity. People from all over the world come there to meditate and pray. On the occasion of his birth centennial in 2014, a second LOTUS was opened at Swami Satchidananda's birthplace in South India.

Swami Satchidananda served on the advisory boards of many Yoga, world peace, and interfaith organizations. Over the years, he received many honors for his humanitarian service, including the Juliet Hollister Award presented at the United Nations and in 2002, the U Thant Peace Award. In 2014, he was posthumously honored as an "interfaith visionary," when the James Parks Morton Interfaith Award was presented by the Interfaith Center of New York.

Swami Satchidananda is the author of numerous books, while his translation and commentary on *The Yoga Sutras of Patanjali*, the foundation of Yoga philosophy, is the best-selling book of its kind. He is also the subject of the documentary, *Living Yoga: The Life and Teachings of Swami Satchidanan*da.

For more information: swamisatchidananda.org and integralyoga.org

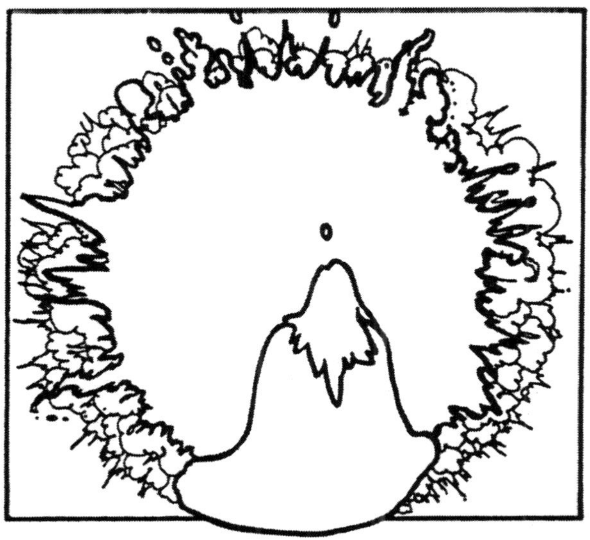

About Peter Max

From visionary pop artist of the 1960s, to master of dynamic neo-Expressionism, Peter Max and his vibrant colors have become part of the fabric of contemporary American culture. In the 1960s Max rose to youthful prominence with his now-famous "Cosmic '60s" style, a bold linear type of painting which depicted transcendental themes. Peter Max revolutionized art of the 1960s just as the Beatles transformed the music of the decade.

Peter Max is a passionate environmentalist and defender of human and animal rights, often dedicating paintings and posters for these noteworthy causes. He has celebrated the principles of freedom and democracy with his famous paintings of American icons of freedom including Lady Liberty and the American Flag.

Peter Max has received many important commissions including the creation of the first "Preserve the Environment" Postage Stamp commemorating the World's Fair in Spokane, Washington; 235 Border Murals at entry points to Canada and Mexico commissioned by the U.S. General Services; and a painting of each of the 50

states, resulting in a book, Peter Max Paints America in celebration of the U.S. Bicentennial. In 1981, he was invited by President and Mrs. Reagan to paint six Liberty portraits at the White House. Max has painted for five U.S. Presidents: Ford, Carter, Reagan, Bush, and Clinton. Max has exhibited in over 40 international museums and over 50 galleries, worldwide.

His work can be found in many prominent museums and private collections around the world, including the Museum of Modern Art in New York City. For more information: petermax.com